THREE NOVELLAS

From the same publishers

Samuel Beckett

Novels

Dream of Fair to Middling Women (1932)
Murphy (1938)
Watt (1945)
First Love (1945)
Mercier and Camier (1946)
Molloy (1951)*
Malone Dies (1951)*

The Unnamable (1953) *
How It Is (1961)
Company (1980)**
Ill Seen Ill Said (1981)**
Worstward Ho (1983)**

* published together as the Trilogy
** published together as Nohow On

Short Prose

More Pricks than Kicks (1934)
Collected Short Prose (in preparation)
Beckett Shorts (see below)

Poetry

Collected Poems (1930-1978)
Anthology of Mexican Poetry
(translations)

Criticism
Proust & Three Dialogues with Georges Duthuit (1931,1949)
Disjecta (1929-1967)

Beckett Shorts (A collection of 12 short volumes to commemorate the writer's death in 1989)
1. Texts for Nothing (1947-52)
2. Dramatic Works and Dialogues (1938-67)
3. All Strange Away (1963)
4. Worstward Ho (1983)
5. Six Residua (1957-72)
6. For to End Yet Again (1960-75)

7. The Old Tune (1962)
8. First Love (1945)
9. As the Story Was Told
10. Three Novellas (1945-6)
11. Stirrings Still (1986-9)
12. Selected Poems (1930-85)

THREE NOVELLAS

Samuel Beckett

John Calder
London

This edition first published 1999 as a collection in Great Britain
by John Calder Publishers
London

The Expelled, *The Calmative* and *The End* originally published by
Les Editions de Minuit, Paris in *Nouvelles et textes pour rien*
1954. First published in Great Britain in 1977 by John Calder
Publishers, London. Republished in *Collected Shorter Prose
1945-1980* in 1984
© All material in this volume Samuel Beckett Estate, 1999
These translations of *The Expelled* and *The End*
© Richard Seaver in collaboration with Samuel Beckett

ISBN 0 7145 43039 Paperback

British Library Cataloguing in Publication Data
A catalogue record for this title is available from the British
Library

Printed by Webcom, Canada

THE EXPELLED

There were not many steps. I had counted them a thousand times, both going up and coming down, but the figure has gone from my mind. I have never known whether you should say one with your foot on the sidewalk, two with the following foot on the first step, and so on, or whether the sidewalk shouldn't count. At the top of the steps I fell foul of the same dilemma. In the other direction, I mean from top to bottom, it was the same, the word is not too strong. I did not know where to begin nor where to end, that's the truth of the matter. I arrived therefore at three totally different figures, without ever knowing which of them was right. And when I say that the figure has gone from my mind, I mean that none of the three figures is with me any more, in my mind. It is true that if I were to find, in my mind, where it is certainly to be found, one of these figures, I would find it and it alone, without being able to deduce from it the other two. And even were I to recover two, I would not know the third. No, I would have to find all three, in my mind, in order to know all three. Memories are killing. So you must not think of certain things, of those that are dear to you, or rather you must think of them, for if you don't there is the danger of finding them, in your mind, little by little. That is to say, you must think of them for a while, a good while, every day several times a day, until they sink forever in the mud. That's an order.

After all it is not the number of steps that matters. The important thing to remember is that there were not many, and that I have remembered. Even for the child there were not many, compared to other steps he knew, from seeing them every day, from going up them and coming down, and playing on them at knuckle-bones and other games the very names of which he has forgotten. What must it have been like then for the man I had overgrown into?

The fall was therefore not serious. Even as I fell I heard the door slam, which brought me a little comfort, in the midst of my fall. For that meant they were not pursuing me down into the street with a stick, to beat me in full view of the passers-by. For if that had been their intention they would not have shut the door, but left it open, so that the persons assembled in the vestibule might enjoy my chastisement and be edified. So, for once, they had confined themselves to throwing me out and no more about it. I had time, before coming to rest in the gutter, to conclude this piece of reasoning.

Under these circumstances nothing compelled me to get up immediately. I rested my elbow on the sidewalk, funny the things you remember, settled my ear in the cup of my hand and began to reflect on my situation, notwithstanding its familiarity. But the sound, fainter but unmistakable, of the door slammed again, roused me from my reverie, in which already a whole landscape was taking form, charming with hawthorn and wild roses, most dreamlike, and made me look up in alarm, my hands flat on the sidewalk and my legs braced for flight. But it was merely my hat sailing towards me through the air, rotating as it came. I caught it and put it on. They were most correct, according to their god. They could have kept this hat, but it was not theirs, it was mine, so they gave it back to me. But the spell was broken.

How describe this hat? And why? When my head had attained I shall not say its definitive but its maximum dimensions, my father said to me, Come, son, we are going to buy your hat, as though it had pre-existed from time immemorial in a pre-established place. He went straight to the hat. I personally had no say in the matter, nor had the hatter. I have often wondered if my father's purpose was not to humiliate me, if he was not jealous of me who was young and handsome, fresh at least, while he was already old and all bloated and purple. It was forbidden me, from that day forth, to go out bareheaded, my pretty brown hair blowing in the wind. Sometimes, in a secluded street, I took it off and held it in my hand, but trembling. I was required to brush it morning and evening. Boys my age with whom, in spite of everything, I was obliged to mix occasionally, mocked me. But I said to myself, It is not really the hat, they simply make merry at the hat because it is a little more glaring than the rest, for they have no finesse. I have always been amazed at my contemporaries' lack of finesse, I whose soul writhed from morning to night, in the mere quest of itself. But perhaps they were simply being kind, like those who make game of the hunchback's big nose. When my father died I could have got rid of this hat, there was nothing more to prevent me, but not I. But how describe it? Some other time, some other time.

I got up and set off. I forget how old I can have been. In what had just happened to me there was nothing in the least memorable. It was neither the cradle nor the grave of anything whatever. Or rather it resembled so many other cradles, so many other graves, that I'm lost. But I don't believe I exaggerate when I say that I was in the prime of life, what I believe is called the

full possession of one's faculties. Ah yes, them I possessed all right. I crossed the street and turned back
towards the house that had just ejected me, I who
never turned back when leaving. How beautiful it was!
There were geraniums in the windows. I have brooded
over geraniums for years. Geraniums are artful
customers, but in the end I was able to do what I liked
with them. I have always greatly admired the door of
this house, up on top of its little flight of steps. How
describe it? It was a massive green door, encased in
summer in a kind of green and white striped housing,
with a hole for the thunderous wrought-iron knocker
and a slit for letters, this latter closed to dust, flies and
tits by a brass flap fitted with springs. So much for
that description. The door was set between two pillars
of the same colour, the bell being on that to the right.
The curtains were in unexceptionable taste. Even the
smoke rising from one of the chimney-pots seemed to
spread and vanish in the air more sorrowful than the
neighbours', and bluer. I looked up at the third and
last floor and saw my window outrageously open. A
thorough cleaning was in full swing. In a few hours
they would close the window, draw the curtains and
spray the whole place with disinfectant. I knew them.
I would have gladly died in that house. In a sort of
vision I saw the door open and my feet come out.

I wasn't afraid to look, for I knew they were not
spying on me from behind the curtains, as they could
have done if they had wished. But I knew them. They
had all gone back into their dens and resumed their
occupations.

And yet I had done them no harm.

I did not know the town very well, scene of my
birth and of my first steps in this world, and then of all
the others, so many that I thought all trace of me was

lost, but I was wrong. I went out so little! Now and then I would go to the window, part the curtains and look out. But then I hastened back to the depths of the room, where the bed was. I felt ill at ease with all this air about me, lost before the confusion of innumerable prospects. But I still knew how to act at this period, when it was absolutely necessary. But first I raised my eyes to the sky, whence cometh our help, where there are no roads, where you wander freely, as in a desert, and where nothing obstructs your vision, wherever you turn your eyes, but the limits of vision itself. When I was younger I thought life would be good in the middle of a plain and went to the Lüneburg heath. With the plain in my head I went to the heath. There were other heaths far less remote, but a voice kept saying to me, It's the Lüneburg heath you need. The element lüne must have had something to do with it. As it turned out the Lüneburg heath was most unsatisfactory, most unsatisfactory. I came home disappointed and at the same time relieved. Yes, I don't know why, but I have never been disappointed, and I often was in the early days, without feeling at the same time, or a moment later, an undeniable relief.

I set off. What a gait. Stiffness of the lower limbs, as if nature had denied me knees, extraordinary splaying of the feet to right and left of the line of march. The trunk, on the contrary, as if by the effect of a compensatory mechanism, was as flabby as an old ragbag, tossing wildly to the unpredictable jolts of the pelvis. I have often tried to correct these defects, to stiffen my bust, flex my knees and walk with my feet in front of one another, for I had at least five or six, but it always ended in the same way, I mean by a loss of equilibrium, followed by a fall. A man must walk without paying attention to what he's doing, as he sighs, and when I walked without paying attention to what I was doing I walked in the way I have just described, and when I began to pay attention I managed a few steps of creditable execution and then fell. I decided therefore to be myself. This carriage is due, in my opinion, in part at least, to a certain leaning from which I have never been able to free myself completely and which left its stamp, as was only to be expected, on my impressionable years, those which govern the fabrication of character, I refer to the period which extends, as far as the eye can see, from the first totterings, behind a chair, to the third form, in which I concluded my studies. I had then the deplorable habit, having pissed in my trousers, or shat there, which I did fairly regularly early in the morning, about ten or half past ten, of persisting in going on and finishing my day as if nothing had happened. The very idea of changing my trousers, or of confiding in mother, who goodness knows asked nothing better than to help me, was unbearable, I don't know why, and till bedtime I dragged on with burning and stinking between my little thighs, or sticking to my bottom, the result of my incontinence. Whence this wary way of walking, with legs stiff and wide apart, and this desperate rolling of the bust, no doubt intended to put people off the scent, to make them think I was full of gaiety and high spirits, without a care in the world, and to lend plausibility to my explanations concerning my nether rigidity, which I ascribed to hereditary rheumatism. My youthful ardour, in so far as I had any, spent itself in this effort, I became sour and mistrustful, a little before my time, in love with hiding and the prone position. Poor juvenile solutions, explaining nothing. No need then for caution, we may reason on to our heart's content, the fog won't lift.

The weather was fine. I advanced down the street, keeping as close as I could to the sidewalk. The widest sidewalk is never wide enough for me, once I set myself in motion, and I hate to inconvenience strangers. A policeman stopped me and said, The street for vehicles, the sidewalk for pedestrians. Like a bit of Old Testament. So I got back on the sidewalk, almost apologetically, and persevered there, in spite of an indescribable jostle, for a good twenty steps, till I had to fling myself to the ground to avoid crushing a child. He was wearing a little harness, I remember, with little bells, he must have taken himself for a pony, or a Clydesdale, why not. I would have crushed him gladly, I loathe children, and it would have been doing him a service, but I was afraid of reprisals. Everyone is a parent, that is what keeps you from hoping. One should reserve, on busy streets, special tracks for these nasty little creatures, their prams, hoops, sweets, scooters, skates, grandpas, grandmas, nannies, balloons and balls, all their foul little happiness in a word. I fell then, and brought down with me an old lady covered with spangles and lace, who must have weighed about sixteen stone. Her screams soon drew a crowd. I had high hopes she had broken her femur, old ladies break their femur easily, but not enough, not enough. I took advantage of the confusion to make off, muttering unintelligible oaths, as if I were the victim, and I was, but I couldn't have proved it. They never lynch children, babies, no matter what they do they are whitewashed in advance. I personally would lynch them with the utmost pleasure, I don't say I'd lend a hand, no, I am not a violent man, but I'd encourage the others and stand them drinks when it was done. But no sooner had I begun to reel on than I was stopped by a second policeman, similar in all respects to the

first, so much so that I wondered whether it was not
the same one. He pointed out to me that the sidewalk
was for everyone, as if it was quite obvious that I
could not be assimilated to that category. Would you
like me, I said, without thinking for a single moment of
Heraclitus, to get down in the gutter? Get down
wherever you want, he said, but leave some room for
others. If you can't bloody well get about like everyone else, he said, you'd do better to stay at home. It
was exactly my feeling. And that he should attribute
to me a home was no small satisfaction. At that moment
a funeral passed, as sometimes happens. There was a
great flurry of hats and at the same time a flutter of
countless fingers. Personally if I were reduced to making
the sign of the cross I would set my heart on doing it
right, nose, navel, left nipple, right nipple. But the
way they did it, slovenly and wild, he seemed crucified
all of a heap, no dignity, his knees under his chin and
his hands anyhow. The more fervent stopped dead
and muttered. As for the policeman he stiffened to
attention, closed his eyes and saluted. Through the
windows of the cabs I caught a glimpse of the mourners
conversing with animation, no doubt scenes from the
life of their late dear brother in Christ, or sister. I seem
to have heard that the hearse trappings are not the
same in both cases, but I never could find out what the
difference consists in. The horses were farting and shit-
ting as if they were going to the fair. I saw no one
kneeling.

But with us the last journey is soon done, it is in
vain you quicken your pace, the last cab containing
the domestics soon leaves you behind, the respite is
over, the bystanders go their ways, you may look to
yourself again. So I stopped a third time, of my own
free will, and entered a cab. Those I had just seen pass,

crammed with people hotly arguing, must have made a strong impression on me. It's a big black box, rocking and swaying on its springs, the windows are small, you curl up in a corner, it smells musty. I felt my hat grazing the roof. A little later I leant forward and closed the windows. Then I sat down again with my back to the horse. I was dozing off when a voice made me start, the cabman's. He had opened the door, no doubt despairing of making himself heard through the window. All I saw was his moustache. Where to? he said. He had climbed down from his seat on purpose to ask me that. And I who thought I was far away already. I reflected, searching in my memory for the name of a street, or a monument. Is your cab for sale? I said. I added, Without the horse. What would I do with a horse? But what would I do with a cab? Could I as much as stretch out in it? Who would bring me food? To the Zoo, I said. It is rare for a capital to be without a Zoo. I added, Don't go too fast. He laughed. The suggestion that he might go too fast to the Zoo must have amused him. Unless it was the prospect of being cabless. Unless it was simply myself, my own person, whose presence in the cab must have transformed it, so much so that the cabman, seeing me there with my head in the shadows of the roof and my knees against the window, had wondered perhaps if it was really his cab, really a cab. He hastens to look at his horse, and is reassured. But does one ever know oneself why one laughs? His laugh in any case was brief, which suggested I was not the joke. He closed the door and climbed back to his seat. It was not long then before the horse got under way.

Yes, surprising though it may seem, I still had a little money at this time. The small sum my father had left me as a gift, with no restrictions, at his death, I still wonder if it wasn't stolen from me. Then I had none. And yet my life went on, and even in the way I wanted, up to a point. The great disadvantage of this condition, which might be defined as the absolute impossibility of all purchase, is that it compels you to bestir yourself. It is rare, for example, when you are completely penniless, that you can have food brought to you from time to time in your retreat. You are therefore obliged to go out and bestir yourself, at least one day a week. You can hardly have a home address under these circumstances, it's inevitable. It was therefore with a certain delay that I learnt they were looking for me, for an affair concerning me. I forget through what channel. I did not read the newspapers, nor do I remember having spoken with anyone during these years, except perhaps three or four times, on the subject of food. At any rate, I must have had wind of the affair one way or another, otherwise I would never have gone to see the lawyer, Mr. Nidder, strange how one fails to forget certain names, and he would never have received me. He verified my identity. That took some time. I showed him the metal initials in the lining of my hat, they proved nothing but they increased the probabilities. Sign, he said. He played with a cylindrical ruler, you could have felled an ox with it. Count, he said. A young woman, perhaps venal, was present at this interview, as a witness no doubt. I stuffed the wad in my pocket. You shouldn't do that, he said. It occurred to me that he should have asked me to count before I signed, it would have been more in order. Where can I reach you, he said, if necessary? At the foot of the stairs I thought of something. Soon after I went back to ask him where this money came from, adding that I had a right to know. He gave me a woman's name that I've forgotten.

Perhaps she had dandled me on her knees while I was still in swaddling clothes and there had been some lovey-dovey. Sometimes that suffices. I repeat, in swaddling clothes, for any later it would have been too late, for lovey-dovey. It is thanks to this money then that I still had a little. Very little. Divided by my life to come it was negligible, unless my conjectures were unduly pessimistic. I knocked on the partition beside my hat, right in the cabman's back if my calculations were correct. A cloud of dust rose from the upholstery. I took a stone from my pocket and knocked with the stone, until the cab stopped. I noticed that, unlike most vehicles, which slow down before stopping, the cab stopped dead. I waited. The whole cab shook. The cabman, on his high seat, must have been listening. I saw the horse as with my eyes of flesh. It had not lapsed into the drooping attitude of its briefest halts, it remained alert, its ears pricked up. I looked out of the window, we were again in motion. I banged again on the partition, until the cab stopped again. The cabman got down cursing from his seat. I lowered the window to prevent his opening the door. Faster, faster. He was redder than ever, purple in other words. Anger, or the rushing wind. I told him I was hiring him for the day. He replied that he had a funeral at three o'clock. Ah the dead. I told him I had changed my mind and no longer wished to go to the Zoo. Let us not go to the Zoo, I said. He replied that it made no difference to him where we went, provided it wasn't too far, because of his beast. And they talk to us about the specificity of primitive peoples' speech. I asked him if he knew of an eating-house. I added, You'll eat with me. I prefer being with a regular customer in such places. There was a long table with two benches of exactly the same length on either side. Across the table he

spoke to me of his life, of his wife, of his beast, then
again of his life, of the atrocious life that was his,
chiefly because of his character. He asked me if I
realized what it meant to be out of doors in all weathers.
I learnt there were still some cabmen who spent their
day snug and warm inside their cabs on the rank,
waiting for a customer to come and rouse them. Such
a thing was possible in the past, but nowadays other
methods were necessary, if a man was to have a little
laid up at the end of his days. I described my situation
to him, what I had lost and what I was looking for. We
did our best, both of us, to understand, to explain. He
understood that I had lost my room and needed
another, but all the rest escaped him. He had taken it
into his head, whence nothing could ever dislodge it,
that I was looking for a furnished room. He took from
his pocket an evening paper of the day before, or
perhaps the day before that again, and proceeded to
run through the advertisements, five or six of which he
underlined with a tiny pencil, the same that hovered
over the likely outsiders. He underlined no doubt
those he would have underlined if he had been in my
shoes, or perhaps those concentrated in the same area,
because of his beast. I would only have confused him
by saying that I could tolerate no furniture in my
room except the bed, and that all the other pieces, and
even the very night-table, had to be removed before I
would consent to set foot in it. About three o'clock we
roused the horse and set off again. The cabman suggested I climb up beside him on the seat, but for some
time already I had been dreaming of the inside of the
cab and I got back inside. We visited, methodically I
hope, one after another, the addresses he had underlined. The short winter's day was drawing to a close.
It seems to me sometimes that these are the only days

I have ever known, and especially that most charming
moment of all, just before night wipes them out. The
addresses he had underlined, or rather marked with a
cross, as common people do, proved fruitless one by
one, and one by one he crossed them out with a
diagonal stroke. Later he showed me the paper,
advising me to keep it safe so as to be sure not to look
again where I had already looked in vain. In spite of
the closed windows, the creaking of the cab and the
traffic noises, I heard him singing, all alone aloft on
his seat. He had preferred me to a funeral, this was a
fact which would endure forever. He sang, *She is far
from the land where her young hero*, those are the only
words I remember. At each stop he got down from his
seat and helped me down from mine. I rang at the
door he directed me to and sometimes I disappeared
inside the house. It was a strange feeling, I remember,
a house all about me again, after so long. He waited
for me on the sidewalk and helped me climb back into
the cab. I was sick and tired of this cabman. He
clambered back to his seat and we set off again. At a
certain moment there occurred this. He stopped. I
shook off my torpor and made ready to get down. But
he did not come to open the door and offer me his arm,
so that I was obliged to get down by myself. He was
lighting the lamps. I love oil lamps, in spite of their
having been, with candles, and if I except the stars, the
first lights I ever knew. I asked him if I might light the
second lamp, since he had already lit the first himself.
He gave me his box of matches, I swung open on its
hinges the little convex glass, lit and closed at once, so
that the wick might burn steady and bright, snug in its
little house, sheltered from the wind. I had this joy.
We saw nothing, by the light of these lamps, save the
vague outlines of the horse, but the others saw them

from afar, two yellow glows sailing slowly through the air. When the equipage turned an eye could be seen, red or green as the case might be, a bossy rhomb, as clear and keen as stained glass.

After we had verified the last address the cabman suggested bringing me to a hotel he knew where I would be comfortable. That makes sense, cabman, hotel, it's plausible. With his recommendation I would want for nothing. Every convenience, he said, with a wink. I place this conversation on the sidewalk, in front of the house from which I had just emerged. I remember, beneath the lamp, the flank of the horse, hollow and damp, and on the handle of the door the cabman's hand in its woollen glove. The roof of the cab was on a level with my neck. I suggested we have a drink. The horse had neither eaten nor drunk all day. I mentioned this to the cabman, who replied that his beast would take no food till it was back in the stable. If it ate anything whatever, during work, were it but an apple or a lump of sugar, it would have stomach pains and colics that would root it to the spot and might even kill it. That was why he was compelled to tie its jaws together with a strap whenever for one reason or another he had to let it out of his sight, so that it would not have to suffer from the kind hearts of the passers-by. After a few drinks the cabman invited me to do his wife and him the honour of spending the night in their home. It was not far. Recollecting these emotions, with the celebrated advantage of tranquillity, it seems to me he did nothing else, all that day, but turn about his lodging. They lived above a stable, at the back of a yard. Ideal location, I could have done with it. Having presented me to his wife, extraordinarily full-bottomed, he left us. She was manifestly ill at ease, alone with me. I could understand her, I don't stand on ceremony on

these occasions. No reason for this to end or go on.
Then let it end. I said I would go down to the stable
and sleep there. The cabman protested. I insisted. He
drew his wife's attention to the pustule on top of my
skull, for I had removed my hat out of civility. He
should have that removed, she said. The cabman
named a doctor he held in high esteem who had
rid him of an induration of the seat. If he wants to
sleep in the stable, said his wife, let him sleep in the
stable. The cabman took the lamp from the table and
preceded me down the stairs, or rather ladder, which
descended to the stable, leaving his wife in the dark. He
spread a horse blanket on the ground in a corner on
the straw and left me a box of matches in case I needed
to see clearly in the night. I don't remember what the
horse was doing all this time. Stretched out in the dark
I heard the noise it made as it drank, a noise like no
other, the sudden gallop of the rats and above me the
muffled voices of the cabman and his wife as they
criticized me. I held the box of matches in my hand,
a big box of safety matches. I got up during the night
and struck one. Its brief flame enabled me to locate the
cab. I was seized, then abandoned, by the desire to set
fire to the stable. I found the cab in the dark, opened
the door, the rats poured out, I climbed in. As I
settled down I noticed that the cab was no longer level,
it was inevitable, with the shafts resting on the ground.
It was better so, that allowed me to lie well back, with
my feet higher than my head on the other seat.
Several times during the night I felt the horse looking
at me through the window and the breath of its
nostrils. Now that it was unharnessed it must have
been puzzled by my presence in the cab. I was cold,
having forgotten to take the blanket, but not quite
enough to go and get it. Through the window of the

cab I saw the window of the stable, more and more clearly. I got out of the cab. It was not so dark now in the stable, I could make out the manger, the rack, the harness hanging, what else, buckets and brushes. I went to the door but couldn't open it. The horse didn't take its eyes off me. Don't horses ever sleep? It seemed to me the cabman should have tied it, to the manger for example. So I was obliged to leave by the window. It wasn't easy. But what is easy? I went out head first, my hands were flat on the ground of the yard while my legs were still thrashing to get clear of the frame. I remember the tufts of grass on which I pulled with both hands, in my effort to extricate myself. I should have taken off my greatcoat and thrown it through the window, but that would have meant thinking of it. No sooner had I left the yard than I thought of something. Weakness. I slipped a banknote in the match-box, went back to the yard and placed the box on the sill of the window through which I had just come. The horse was at the window. But after I had taken a few steps in the street I returned to the yard and took back my banknote. I left the matches, they were not mine. The horse was still at the window. I was sick and tired of this cabhorse. Dawn was just breaking. I did not know where I was. I made towards the rising sun, towards where I thought it should rise, the quicker to come into the light. I would have liked a sea horizon, or a desert one. When I am abroad in the morning I go to meet the sun, and in the evening, when I am abroad, I follow it, till I am down among the dead. I don't know why I told this story. I could just as well have told another. Perhaps some other time I'll be able to tell another. Living souls, you will see how alike they are.

Translated by RICHARD SEAVER
in collaboration with the author

THE CALMATIVE
Translated by Samuel Beckett

THE CALMATIVE

I don't know when I died. It always seemed to me
I died old, about ninety years old, and what years, and
that my body bore it out, from head to foot. But this
evening, alone in my icy bed, I have the feeling I'll be
older than the day, the night, when the sky with all its
lights fell upon me, the same I had so often gazed on
since my first stumblings on the distant earth. For I'm
too frightened this evening to listen to myself rot,
waiting for the great red lapses of the heart, the
tearings at the caecal walls, and for the slow killings to
finish in my skull, the assaults on unshakable pillars,
the fornications with corpses. So I'll tell myself a story,
I'll try and tell myself another story, to try and calm
myself, and it's there I feel I'll be old, old, even older
than the day I fell, calling for help, and it came. Or is it
possible that in this story I have come back to life, after
my death? No, it's not like me to come back to life,
after my death.

What possessed me to stir when I wasn't with anybody? Was I being thrown out? No, I wasn't with
anybody. I see a kind of den littered with empty tins.
And yet we are not in the country. Perhaps it's just
ruins, a ruined folly, on the skirts of the town, in a field,
for the fields come right up to our walls, their walls,
and the cows lie down at night in the lee of the ramparts. I have changed refuge so often, in the course of
my rout, that now I can't tell between dens and ruins.
But there was never any city but the one. It is true

you often move along in a dream, houses and factories
darken the air, trams go by and under your feet wet
from the grass there are suddenly cobbles. I only know
the city of my childhood, I must have seen the other,
but unbelieving. All I say cancels out, I'll have said
nothing. Was I hungry itself? Did the weather tempt
me? It was cloudy and cool, I insist, but not to the
extent of luring me out. I couldn't get up at the first
attempt, nor let us say at the second, and once up,
propped against the wall, I wondered if I could go on,
I mean up, propped against the wall. Impossible to go
out and walk. I speak as though it all happened yesterday. Yesterday indeed is recent, but not enough. For
what I tell this evening is passing this evening, at this
passing hour. I'm no longer with these assassins, in
this bed of terror, but in my distant refuge, my hands
twined together, my head bowed, weak, breathless,
calm, free, and older than I'll have ever been, if my
calculations are correct. I'll tell my story in the past
none the less, as though it were a myth, or an old fable,
for this evening I need another age, that age to become
another age in which I became what I was.

But little by little I got myself out and started walking with short steps among the trees, oh look, trees!
The paths of other days were rank with tangled growth.
I leaned against the trunks to get my breath and pulled
myself forward with the help of boughs. Of my last
passage no trace remained. They were the perishing
oaks immortalized by d'Aubigné. It was only a grove.
The fringe was near, a light less green and kind of
tattered told me so, in a whisper. Yes, no matter where
you stood, in this little wood, and were it in the furthest
recess of its poor secrecies, you saw on every hand the
gleam of this pale light, promise of God knows what
fatuous eternity. Die without too much pain, a little,

that's worth your while. Under the blind sky close with
your own hands the eyes soon sockets, then quick into
carrion not to mislead the crows. That's the advantage
of death by drowning, one of the advantages, the crabs
never get there too soon. But here a strange thing, I
was no sooner free of the wood at last, having crossed
unminding the ditch that girdles it, than thoughts
came to me of cruelty, the kind that smiles. A lush
pasture lay before me, nonsuch perhaps, who cares,
drenched in evening dew or recent rain. Beyond this
meadow to my certain knowledge a path, then a field
and finally the ramparts, closing the prospect. Cyclo-
pean and crenellated, standing out faintly against a
sky scarcely less sombre, they did not seem in ruins,
viewed from mine, but were, to my certain knowledge.
Such was the scene offered to me, in vain, for I knew it
well and loathed it. What I saw was a bald man in a
brown suit, a comedian. He was telling a funny story
about a fiasco. Its point escaped me. He used the word
snail, or slug, to the delight of all present. The women
seemed even more entertained than their escorts, if that
were possible. Their shrill laughter pierced the clapping
and, when this had subsided, broke out still here and
there in sudden peals even after the next story had
begun, so that part of it was lost. Perhaps they had in
mind the reigning penis sitting who knows by their
side and from that sweet shore launched their cries of
joy towards the comic vast, what a talent. But it's to
me this evening something has to happen, to my body
as in myth and metamorphosis, this old body to which
nothing ever happened, or so little, which never met
with anything, loved anything, wished for anything, in
its tarnished universe, except for the mirrors to shatter,
the plane, the curved, the magnifying, the minifying,
and to vanish in the havoc of its images. Yes, this

evening it has to be as in the story my father used to
read to me, evening after evening, when I was small,
and he had all his health, to calm me, evening after
evening, year after year it seems to me this evening,
which I don't remember much about, except that it
was the adventures of one Joe Breem, or Breen, the
son of a lighthouse-keeper, a strong muscular lad of
fifteen, those were the words, who swam for miles in
the night, a knife between his teeth, after a shark, I
forget why, out of sheer heroism. He might have
simply told me the story, he knew it by heart, so did I,
but that wouldn't have calmed me, he had to read it
to me, evening after evening, or pretend to read it to
me, turning the pages and explaining the pictures that
were of me already, evening after evening the same
pictures till I dozed off on his shoulder. If he had
skipped a single word I would have hit him, with my
little fist, in his big belly bursting out of the old
cardigan and unbuttoned trousers that rested him from
his office canonicals. For me now the setting forth, the
struggle and perhaps the return, for the old man I am
this evening, older than my father ever was, older than
I shall ever be. I crossed the meadow with little stiff
steps at the same time limp, the best I could manage.
Of my last passage no trace remained, it was long ago.
And the little bruised stems soon straighten up again,
having need of air and light, and as for the broken
their place is soon taken. I entered the town by what
they call the Shepherds' Gate without having seen a
soul, only the first bats like flying crucifixions, nor heard
a sound except my steps, my heart in my breast and
then, as I went under the arch, the hoot of an owl,
that cry at once so soft and fierce which in the night,
calling, answering, through my little wood and those
nearby, sounded in my shelter like a tocsin. The

further I went into the city the more I was struck by its deserted air. It was lit as usual, brighter than usual, although the shops were shut. But the lights were on in their windows with the object no doubt of attracting customers and prompting them to say, I say, I like that, not dear either, I'll come back tomorrow, if I'm still alive. I nearly said, Good God it's Sunday. The trams were running, the buses too, but few, slow, empty, noiseless, as if under water. I didn't see a single horse! I was wearing my long green greatcoat with the velvet collar, such as motorists wore about 1900, my father's, but that day it was sleeveless, a vast cloak. But on me it was still the same great dead weight, with no warmth to it, and the tails swept the ground, scraped it rather, they had grown so stiff, and I so shrunken. What would, what could happen to me in this empty place? But I felt the houses packed with people, lurking behind the curtains they looked out into the street or, crouched far back in the depths of the room, head in hands, were sunk in dream. Up aloft my hat, the same as always, I reached no further. I went right across the city and came to the sea, having followed the river to its mouth. I kept saying, I'll go back, unbelieving. The boats at anchor in the harbour, tied up to the jetty, seemed no less numerous than usual, as if I knew anything about what was usual. But the quays were deserted and there was no sign or stir of arrival or departure. But all might change from one moment to the next and be transformed like magic before my eyes. Then all the bustle of the people and things of the sea, the masts of the big craft gravely rocking and of the small more jauntily, I insist, and I'd hear the gulls' terrible cry and perhaps the sailors' cry. And I might slip unnoticed aboard a freighter outward bound and get far away and spend far away a few good months,

perhaps even a year or two, in the sun, in peace, before
I died. And without going that far it would be a sad
state of affairs if in that unscandalizable throng I
couldn't achieve a little encounter that would calm me
a little, or exchange a few words with a navigator for
example, words to carry away with me to my refuge, to
add to my collection. I waited sitting on a kind of top-
less capstan, saying, The very capstans this evening are
out of order. And I gazed out to sea, out beyond the
breakwaters, without sighting the least vessel. I could
see lights flush with the water. And the pretty beacons
at the harbour mouth I could see too, and others in the
distance, flashing from the coast, the islands, the head-
lands. But seeing still no sign or stir I made ready to go,
to turn away sadly from this dead haven, for there are
scenes that call for strange farewells. I had merely to
bow my head and look down at my feet, for it is in this
attitude I always drew the strength to, how shall I say,
I don't know, and it was always from the earth, rather
than from the sky, notwithstanding its reputation, that
my help came in time of trouble. And there, on the
flagstone, which I was not focusing, for why focus it, I
saw haven afar, where the black swell was most peril-
ous, and all about me storm and wreck. I'll never
come back here, I said. But when with a thrust of both
hands against the rim of the capstan I heaved myself
up I found facing me a young boy holding a goat by a
horn. I sat down again. He stood there silent looking at
me without visible fear or revulsion. Admittedly the
light was poor. His silence seemed natural to me, it
befitted me as the elder to speak first. He was barefoot
and in rags. Haunter of the waterfront he had stepped
aside to see what the dark hulk could be abandoned on
the quayside. Such was my train of thought. Close up
to me now with his little guttersnipe's eye there could

be no doubt left in his mind. And yet he stayed. Can this base thought be mine? Moved, for after all that is what I must have come out for, in a way, and with little expectation of advantage from what might follow, I resolved to speak to him. So I marshalled the words and opened my mouth, thinking I would hear them. But all I heard was a kind of rattle, unintelligible even to me who knew what was intended. But it was nothing, mere speechlessness due to long silence, as in the wood that darkens the mouth of hell, do you remember, I only just. Without letting go of his goat he moved right up against me and offered me a sweet out of a twist of paper such as you could buy for a penny. I hadn't been offered a sweet for eighty years at least, but I took it eagerly and put it in my mouth, the old gesture came back to me, more and more moved since that is what I wanted. The sweets were stuck together and I had my work cut out to separate the top one, a green one, from the others, but he helped me and his hand brushed mine. And a moment later as he made to move away, hauling his goat after him, with a great gesticulation of my whole body I motioned him to stay and I said, in an impetuous murmur, Where are you off to, my little man, with your nanny? The words were hardly out of my mouth when for shame I covered my face. And yet they were the same I had tried to utter but a moment before. Where are you off to, my little man, with your nanny! If I could have blushed I would have, but there was not enough blood left in my extremities. If I had had a penny in my pocket I would have given it to him, for him to forgive me, but I did not have a penny in my pocket, nor anything resembling it. Nothing that could give pleasure to a little unfortunate at the mouth of life. I suspect I had nothing with me but my stone, that day,

having gone out as it were without premeditation. Of
his little person I was fated to see no more than the
black curly hair and the pretty curve of the long bare
legs all muscle and dirt. And the hand, so fresh and
keen, I would not forget in a hurry either. I looked for
better words to say to him, I found them too late, he
was gone, oh not far, but far. Out of my life too he
went without a care, not one of his thoughts would
ever be for me again, unless perhaps when he was old
and, delving in his boyhood, would come upon that
gallows night and hold the goat by the horn again and
linger again a moment by my side, with who knows
perhaps a touch of tenderness, even of envy, but I have
my doubts. Poor dear dumb beasts, how you will have
helped me. What does your daddy do? that's what I
would have said to him if he had given me the chance.
Soon they were no more than a single blur which if I
hadn't known I might have taken for a young centaur.
I was nearly going to have the goat dung, then pick up
a handful of the pellets so soon cold and hard, sniff
and even taste them, no, that would not help me this
evening. I say this evening as if it were always the same
evening, but are there two evenings? I went, in-
tending to get back as fast as I could, but it would not
be quite empty-handed, repeating, I'll never come back
here. My legs were paining me, every step would
gladly have been the last, but the glances I darted towards the windows, stealthily, showed me a great
cylinder sweeping past as though on rollers on the
asphalt. I must indeed have been moving fast, for I
overhauled more than one pedestrian, there are the
first men, without extending myself, I who in the
normal way was left standing by cripples, and then I
seemed to hear the footfalls die behind me. And yet
each little step would gladly have been the last. So

much so that when I emerged on a square I hadn't
noticed on the way out, with a cathedral looming on
the far side, I decided to go in, if it was open, and hide,
as in the Middle Ages, for a space. I say cathedral, it
may not have been, I don't know, all I know is it would
vex me in this story that aspires to be the last, to have
taken refuge in a common church. I remarked the
Saxon Stützenwechsel. Charming effect, but it didn't
charm me. The brilliantly lit nave appeared deserted.
I walked round it several times without seeing a soul.
They were hiding perhaps, under the choir-stalls, or
dodging behind the pillars, like woodpeckers. Suddenly
close to where I was, and without my having heard
the long preliminary rumblings, the organ began to
boom. I sprang up from the mat on which I lay before
the altar and hastened to the far end of the nave as if
on my way out. But it was a side aisle and the door I
disappeared through was not the exit. For instead of
being restored to the night I found myself at the foot of
a spiral staircase which I began to climb at top speed,
mindless of my heart, like one hotly pursued by a
homicidal maniac. This staircase faintly lit by I know
not what means, slits perhaps, I mounted panting as
far as the projecting gallery in which it culminated and
which, separated from the void by a cynical parapet,
encompassed a smooth round wall capped by a little
dome covered with lead or verdigrised copper, phew,
if that's not clear. People must have come here for the
view, those who fall die on the way. Flattening myself
against the wall I started round, clockwise. But I had
hardly gone a few steps when I met a man revolving in
the other direction, with the utmost circumspection.
How I'd love to push him, or him to push me, over the
edge. He gazed at me wild-eyed for a moment and
then, not daring to pass me on the parapet side and

surmising correctly that I would not relinquish the
wall just to oblige him, abruptly turned his back on
me, his head rather, for his back remained glued to the
wall, and went back the way he had come so that soon
there was nothing left of him but a left hand. It lingered
a moment, then slid out of sight. All that remained to
me was the vision of two burning eyes starting out of
their sockets under a check cap. Into what nightmare thingness am I fallen? My hat flew off, but did
not get far thanks to the string. I turned my head towards the staircase and lent an eye. Nothing. Then a
little girl came into view followed by a man holding
her by the hand, both pressed against the wall. He
pushed her into the stairway, disappeared after her,
turned and raised towards me a face that made me
recoil. I could only see his bare head above the top
step. When they were gone I called. I completed in
haste the round of the gallery. No one. I saw on the
horizon, where sky, sea, plain and mountain meet, a
few low stars, not to be confused with the fires men
light, at night, or that go alight alone. Enough. Back
in the street I tried to find my way in the sky, where I
knew the Bears so well. If I had seen someone I would
have stopped him to ask, the most ferocious aspect
would not have daunted me. I would have said,
touching my hat, Pardon me your honour, the
Shepherds' Gate for the love of God. I thought I could
go no further, but no sooner had the impetus reached
my legs than on I went, believe it or not, at a very fair
pace. I wasn't returning empty-handed, not quite, I
was taking back with me the virtual certainty that I
was still of this world, of that world too, in a way. But
I was paying the price. I would have done better to
spend the night in the cathedral, on the mat before the
altar, I would have continued on my way at first light,

or they would have found me stretched out in the
rigor of death, the genuine bodily article, under the
blue eyes fount of so much hope, and put me in the
evening papers. But suddenly I was descending a wide
street, vaguely familiar, but in which I could never
have set foot, in my lifetime. But soon realizing I was
going downhill I turned about and set off in the other
direction. For I was afraid if I went downhill of returning to the sea where I had sworn never to return.
When I say I turned about I mean I wheeled round in
a wide semicircle without slowing down, for I was
afraid if I stopped of not being able to start again, yes,
I was afraid of that too. And this evening too I dare
not stop. I was struck more and more by the contrast
between the brightly lit streets and their deserted air.
To say it distressed me, no, but I say it all the same,
in the hope of calming myself. To say there was no
one abroad, no, I would not go that far, for I remarked
a number of shapes, male and female, strange shapes,
but not more so than usual. As to what hour it might
have been I had no idea, except that it must have been
some hour of the night. But it might have been three
or four in the morning just as it might have been ten
or eleven in the evening, depending no doubt on
whether one wondered at the scarcity of passers-by or
at the extraordinary radiance shed by the street-lamps
and traffic-lights. For at one or other of these no one
could fail to wonder, unless he was out of his mind.
Not a single private car, but admittedly from time to
time a public vehicle, slow sweep of light silent and
empty. It is not my wish to labour these antinomies,
for we are needless to say in a skull, but I have no
choice but to add the following few remarks. All the
mortals I saw were alone and as if sunk in themselves.
It must be a common sight, but mixed with something

else I imagine. The only couple was two men grappling, their legs intertwined. I only saw one cyclist! He was going the same way as I was. All were going the same way as I was, vehicles too, I have only just realized it. He was pedalling slowly in the middle of the street, reading a newspaper which he held with both hands spread open before his eyes. Every now and then he rang his bell without interrupting his reading. I watched him recede till he was no more than a dot on the horizon. Suddenly a young woman perhaps of easy virtue, dishevelled and her dress in disarray, darted across the street like a rabbit. That is all I had to add. But here a strange thing, yet another, I had no pain whatever, not even in my legs. Weakness. A good night's nightmare and a tin of sardines would restore my sensitivity. My shadow, one of my shadows, flew before me, dwindled, slid under my feet, trailed behind me the way shadows will. This degree of opacity appeared to me conclusive. But suddenly ahead of me a man on the same side of the street and going the same way, to keep harping on the same thing lest I forget. The distance between us was considerable, seventy paces at least, and fearing he might escape me I quickened my step with the result I swept forward as if on rollers. This is not me, I said, let us make the most of it. Finding myself in an instant a bare ten paces in his rear I slowed down so as not to burst in on him and so heighten the aversion my person inspired even in its most abject and obsequious attitudes. And a moment later, keeping humbly in step with him, Excuse me your honour, the Shepherds' Gate for the love of God! At close quarters he appeared normal apart from that air already noted of ebbing inward. I drew a few steps ahead, turned, cringed, touched my hat and said, The right time for mercy's sake! I might as well not have

existed. But what about the sweet? A light! I cried.
Given my need of help I can't think why I did not bar
his path. I couldn't have, that's all, I couldn't have
touched him. Seeing a stone seat by the kerb I sat down
and crossed my legs, like Walther. I must have dozed
off, for the next thing was a man sitting beside me. I
was still taking him in when he opened his eyes and set
them on me, as if for the first time, for he shrank back
unaffectedly. Where did you spring from? he said. To
hear myself addressed again so soon impressed me
greatly. What's the matter with you? he said. I tried
to look like one with whom that only is the matter
which is native to him. Forgive me your honour, I said,
gingerly lifting my hat and rising a fraction from the
seat, the right time for the love of God! He said a time,
I don't remember which, a time that explained nothing,
that's all I remember, and did not calm me. But what
time could have done that? Oh I know, I know, one
will come that will. But in the meantime? What's that
you said? he said. Unfortunately I had said nothing.
But I wriggled out of it by asking him if he could help
me find my way which I had lost. No, he said, for I am
not from these parts and if I am sitting on this slab it
is because the hotels were full or would not let me in,
I have no opinion. But tell me the story of your life,
then we'll see. My life! I cried. Why yes, he said, you
know, that kind of—what shall I say? He brooded for
a time, no doubt trying to think of what life could well
be said to be a kind. In the end he went on, testily,
Come now, everyone knows that. He jogged me in the
ribs. No details, he said, the main drift, the main drift.
But as I remained silent he said, Shall I tell you mine,
then you'll see what I mean. The account he then gave
was brief and dense, facts, without comment. That's
what I call a life, he said, do you follow me now? It

wasn't bad, his story, positively fairy-like in places.
But that Pauline, I said, are you still with her? I am,
he said, but I'm going to leave her and set up with
another, younger and plumper. You travel a lot, I said.
Oh widely, widely, he said. Words were coming back
to me and the way to make them sound. All that's a
thing of the past for you no doubt, he said. Do you
think of spending some time among us? I said. This
sentence struck me as particularly well turned. If it's
not a rude question, he said, how old are you? I don't
know, I said. You don't know! he cried. Not exactly,
I said. Are thighs much in your thoughts, he said,
arses, cunts and environs? I didn't follow. No more
erections naturally, he said. Erections? I said. The
penis, he said, you know what the penis is, there,
between the legs. Ah that! I said. It thickens, lengthens,
stiffens and rises, he said, does it not? I assented,
though they were not the terms I would have used.
That is what we call an erection, he said. He pondered,
then exclaimed, Phenomenal! No? Strange right
enough, I said. And there you have it all, he said. But
what will become of her? I said. Who? he said.
Pauline, I said. She will grow old, he said with tranquil
assurance, slowly at first, then faster and faster, in
pain and bitterness, pulling the devil by the tail. The
face was not full, but I eyed it in vain, it remained
clothed in its flesh instead of turning all chalky and
channelled as with a gouge. The very vomer kept its
cushion. It is true discussion was always bad for me. I
longed for the tender nonsuch, I would have trodden
it gently, with my boots in my hand, and for the shade
of my wood, far from this terrible light. What are you
grinning and bearing? he said. He held on his knees a
big black bag, like a midwife's I imagine. It was full
of glittering phials. I asked him if they were all alike.

Oho no, he said, for every taste. He took one and held it out to me, saying, One and six. What did he want? To sell it to me? Proceeding on this hypothesis I told him I had no money. No money! he cried. All of a sudden his hand came down on the back of my neck, his sinewy fingers closed and with a jerk and a twist he had me up against him. But instead of dispatching me he began to murmur words so sweet that I went limp and my head fell forward in his lap. Between the caressing voice and the fingers rowelling my neck the contrast was striking. But gradually the two things merged in a devastating hope, if I dare say so, and I dare. For this evening I have nothing to lose that I can discern. And if I have reached this point (in my story) without anything having changed, for if anything had changed I think I'd know, the fact remains I have reached it, and that's something, and with nothing changed, and that's something too. It's no excuse for rushing matters. No, it must cease gently, as gently cease on the stairs the steps of the loved one, who could not love and will not come back, and whose steps say so, that she could not love and will not come back. He suddenly shoved me away and showed me the phial again. There you have it all, he said. It can't have been the same all as before. Want it? he said. No, but I said yes, so as not to vex him. He proposed an exchange. Give me your hat, he said. I refused. What vehemence! he said. I haven't a thing, I said. Try in your pockets, he said. I haven't a thing, I said, I came out without a thing. Give me a lace, he said. I refused. Long silence. And if you gave me a kiss, he said finally. I knew there were kisses in the air. Can you take off your hat? he said. I took it off. Put it back, he said, you look nicer with it on. I put it back. Come on, he said, give me a kiss and let there be an end to it. Did it not occur to him

I might turn him down? No, a kiss is not a bootlace, he must have seen from my face that all passion was not quite spent. Come, he said. I wiped my mouth in its tod of hair and advanced it towards his. Just a moment, he said. My mouth stood still. You know what a kiss is? he said. Yes yes, I said. If it's not a rude question, he said, when was your last? Some time ago, I said, but I can still do them. He took off his hat, a bowler, and tapped the middle of his forehead. There, he said, and there only. He had a noble brow, white and high. He leaned forward, closing his eyes. Quick, he said. I pursed up my lips as mother had taught me and brought them down where he had said. Enough, he said. He raised his hand to the spot, but left the gesture unfinished and put on his hat. I turned away and looked across the street. It was then I noticed we were sitting opposite a horse-butcher's. Here, he said, take it. I had forgotten. He rose. Standing he was quite short. One good turn, he said, with radiant smile. His teeth shone. I listened to his steps die away. How tell what remains? But it's the end. Or have I been dreaming, am I dreaming? No no, none of that, for dream is nothing, a joke, and significant what is worse. I said, Stay where you are till day breaks, wait sleeping till the lamps go out and the streets come to life. But I stood up and moved off. My pains were back, but with something untoward which prevented my wrapping them round me. But I said, Little by little you are coming to. From my gait alone, slow, stiff and which seemed at every step to solve a stato-dynamic problem never posed before, I would have been known again, if I had been known. I crossed over and stopped before the butcher's. Behind the grille the curtains were drawn, rough canvas curtains striped blue and white, colours of the Virgin, and stained with great pink stains. They did not quite meet in the middle and through the chink I could make out the dim carcasses of the gutted horses hanging from hooks head downwards. I hugged the walls, famished for shadow. To think that in a moment all will be said, all to do again. And the city clocks, what was wrong with them, whose great chill clang even in my wood fell on me from the air? What else? Ah yes, my spoils. I tried to think of Pauline, but she eluded me, gleamed an instant and was gone, like the young woman in the street. So I went in the atrocious brightness, bedded in my old flesh, straining towards an issue and passing them by to left and right and my mind panting after this and that and always flung back to where there was nothing. I succeeded however in fastening briefly on the little girl, long enough to see her a little more clearly than before, so that she wore a kind of bonnet and clasped in her hand a book, of common prayer perhaps, and to try and have her smile, but she did not smile, but vanished down the staircase without having yielded me her little face. I had to stop. At first nothing, then little by little, I mean rising up out of the silence till suddenly no higher, a kind of massive murmur coming perhaps from the house that was propping me up. That reminded me that the houses were full of people, besieged, no, I don't know. When I stepped back to look at the windows I could see, in spite of shutters, blinds and muslins, that many of the rooms were lit. The light was so dimmed by the brilliancy flooding the boulevard that short of knowing or suspecting it was not so one might have supposed everyone sleeping. The sound was not continuous, but broken by silences possibly of consternation. I thought of ringing at the door and asking for shelter and protection till morning. But suddenly I was on my way again. But little by little, in a slow swoon, darkness fell about me. I saw a mass of bright flowers fade in an exquisite cascade of paling colours. I found myself admiring, all along the housefronts, the gradual blossoming of squares and rectangles, casement and sash, yellow, green, pink, according to the curtains and blinds, finding that pretty. Then at last, before I fell, first to my knees, as cattle do, then on my face, I was in a throng. I didn't lose consciousness, when I lose consciousness it will not be to recover it. They paid no heed to me, though careful not to walk on me, a courtesy that must have touched me, it was what I had come out for. It was well with me, sated with dark and calm, lying at the feet of mortals, fathom deep in the grey of dawn, if it was dawn. But reality, too tired to look for the right word, was soon restored, the throng fell away, the light came back and I had no need to raise my head from the ground to know I was back in the same blinding void as before. I said, Stay where you are, down on the friendly stone, or at least indifferent, don't open your eyes, wait for morning. But up with me again and back on the way that was not mine, on uphill along the boulevard. A blessing he was not waiting for me, poor old Breem, or Breen. I said, The sea is east, it's west I must go, to the left of north. But in vain I raised without hope my eyes to the sky to look for the Bears. For the light I steeped in put out the stars, assuming they were there, which I doubted, remembering the clouds.

Translated by the author

THE END
Translated by Richard Seaver
in collaboration with Samuel Beckett

THE END

They clothed me and gave me money. I knew what the money was for, it was to get me started. When it was gone I would have to get more, if I wanted to go on. The same for the shoes, when they were worn out I would have to get them mended, or get myself another pair, or go on barefoot, if I wanted to go on. The same for the coat and trousers, needless to say, with this difference, that I could go on in my shirt-sleeves, if I wanted. The clothes—shoes, socks, trousers, shirt, coat, hat—were not new, but the deceased must have been about my size. That is to say, he must have been a little shorter, a little thinner, for the clothes did not fit me so well in the beginning as they did at the end, the shirt especially, and it was many a long day before I could button it at the neck, or profit by the collar that went with it, or pin the tails together between my legs in the way my mother had taught me. He must have put on his Sunday best to go to the consultation, perhaps for the first time, unable to bear it any longer. Be that as it may the hat was a bowler, in good shape. I said, Keep your hat and give me back mine. I added, Give me back my greatcoat. They replied that they had burnt them, together with my other clothes. I understood then that the end was near, at least fairly near. Later on I tried to exchange this hat for a cap, or a slouch which could be pulled down over my face, but without much success. And yet I could not go about bare-headed, with my skull in the state it

was. At first this hat was too small, then it got used to
me. They gave me a tie, after long discussion. It seemed
a pretty tie to me, but I didn't like it. When it came at
last I was too tired to send it back. But in the end it
came in useful. It was blue, with kinds of little stars.
I didn't feel well, but they told me I was well enough.
They didn't say in so many words that I was as well as
I would ever be, but that was the implication. I lay
inert on the bed and it took three women to put on my
trousers. They didn't seem to take much interest in my
private parts which to tell the truth were nothing to
write home about, I didn't take much interest in them
myself. But they might have passed some remark.
When they had finished I got up and finished dressing
unaided. They told me to sit on the bed and wait. All
the bedding had disappeared. It made me angry that
they had not let me wait in the familiar bed, instead of
leaving me standing in the cold, in these clothes that
smelt of sulphur. I said, You might have left me in the
bed till the last moment. Men all in white came in with
mallets in their hands. They dismantled the bed and
took away the pieces. One of the women followed
them out and came back with a chair which she set
before me. I had done well to pretend I was angry. But
to make it quite clear to them how angry I was that
they had not left me in my bed I gave the chair a kick
that sent it flying. A man came in and made a sign to me
to follow him. In the hall he gave me a paper to sign.
What's this, I said, a safe-conduct? It's a receipt, he
said, for the clothes and money you have received.
What money? I said. It was then I received the money.
To think I had almost departed without a penny in
my pocket. The sum was not large, compared to other
sums, but to me it seemed large. I saw the familiar
objects, companions of so many bearable hours. The

stool, for example, dearest of all. The long afternoons
together, waiting for it to be time for bed. At times I
felt its wooden life invade me, till I myself became a
piece of old wood. There was even a hole for my cyst.
Then the window pane with the patch of frosting gone,
where I used to press my eye in the hour of need, and
rarely in vain. I am greatly obliged to you, I said, is
there a law which prevents you from throwing me out
naked and penniless? That would damage our reputation in the long run, he replied. Could they not
possibly keep me a little longer, I said, I could make
myself useful. Useful, he said, joking apart you would
be willing to make yourself useful? A moment later he
went on, If they believed you were really willing to
make yourself useful they would keep you, I am sure.
The number of times I had said I was going to make
myself useful, I wasn't going to start that again. How
weak I felt! Perhaps, I said, they would consent to
take back the money and keep me a little longer. This
is a charitable institution, he said, and the money is a
gift you receive when you leave. When it is gone you
will have to get more, if you want to go on. Never
come back here whatever you do, you would not be let
in. Don't go to any of our branches either, they would
turn you away. Exelmans! I cried. Come come, he
said, and anyway no one understands a tenth of what
you say. I'm so old, I said. You are not so old as all
that, he said. May I stay here just a little longer, I said,
till the rain is over? You may wait in the cloister, he
said, the rain will go on all day. You may wait in the
cloister till six o'clock, you will hear the bell. If anyone
challenges you, you need only say you have permission
to shelter in the cloister. Whose name will I give? I
said. Weir, he said.

I had not been long in the cloister when the rain stop-

ped and the sun came out. It was low and I reckoned
it must be getting on for six, considering the season. I
stayed there looking through the archway at the sun
as it went down behind the cloister. A man appeared
and asked me what I was doing. What do you want?
were the words he used. Very friendly. I replied that I
had Mr. Weir's permission to stay in the cloister till
six o'clock. He went away, but came back immediately.
He must have spoken to Mr. Weir in the interim, for
he said, You must not loiter in the cloister now the
rain is over.

Now I was making my way through the garden.
There was that strange light which follows a day of
persistent rain, when the sun comes out and the sky
clears too late to be of any use. The earth makes a
sound as of sighs and the last drops fall from the
emptied cloudless sky. A small boy, stretching out his
hands and looking up at the blue sky, asked his mother
how such a thing was possible. Fuck off, she said. I
suddenly remembered I had not thought of asking
Mr. Weir for a piece of bread. He would surely have
given it to me. I had as a matter of fact thought of it
during our conversation in the hall, I had said to myself, Let us first finish our conversation, then I'll ask. I
knew well they would not keep me. I would gladly have
turned back, but I was afraid one of the guards would
stop me and tell me I would never see Mr. Weir again.
That might have added to my sorrow. And anyway I
never turned back on such occasions.

In the street I was lost. I had not set foot in this part
of the city for a long time and it seemed greatly changed.
Whole buildings had disappeared, the palings had
changed position and on all sides I saw, in great
letters, the names of tradesmen I had never seen before
and would have been at a loss to pronounce. There

were streets where I remembered none, some I did remember had vanished and others had completely changed their names. The general impression was the same as before. It is true I did not know the city very well. Perhaps it was quite a different one. I did not know where I was supposed to be going. I had the great good fortune, more than once, not to be run over. My appearance still made people laugh, with that hearty jovial laugh so good for the health. By keeping the red part of the sky as much as possible on my right hand I came at last to the river. Here all seemed at first sight more or less as I had left it. But if I had looked more closely I would doubtless have discovered many changes. And indeed I subsequently did so. But the general appearance of the river, flowing between its quays and under its bridges, had not changed. Yes, the river still gave the impression it was flowing in the wrong direction. That's all a pack of lies I feel. My bench was still there. It was shaped to fit the curves of the seated body. It stood beside a watering trough, gift of a Mrs. Maxwell to the city horses, according to the inscription. During the short time I rested there several horses took advantage of this monument. The iron shoes approached and the jingle of the harness. Then silence. That was the horse looking at me. Then the noise of pebbles and mud that horses make when drinking. Then the silence again. That was the horse looking at me again. Then the pebbles again. Then the silence again. Till the horse had finished drinking or the driver deemed it had drunk its fill. The horses were uneasy. Once, when the noise stopped, I turned and saw the horse looking at me. The driver too was looking at me. Mrs. Maxwell would have been pleased if she could have seen her trough rendering such services to

the city horses. When it was night, after a tedious
twilight, I took off my hat which was paining me. I
longed to be under cover again, in an empty place,
close and warm, with artificial light, an oil lamp for
choice, with a pink shade for preference. From time
to time someone would come to make sure I was all
right and needed nothing. It was long since I had
longed for anything and the effect on me was horrible.

In the days that followed I visited several lodgings,
without much success. They usually slammed the door
in my face, even when I showed my money and offered
to pay a week in advance, or even two. It was in vain I
put on my best manners, smiled and spoke distinctly,
they slammed the door in my face before I could even
finish my little speech. It was at this time I perfected a
method of doffing my hat at once courteous and dis-
creet, neither servile nor insolent. I slipped it smartly
forward, held it a second poised in such a way that the
person addressed could not see my skull, then slipped
it back. To do that naturally, without creating an
unfavourable impression, is no easy matter. When I
deemed that to tip-my hat would suffice, I naturally
did no more than tip it. But to tip one's hat is no easy
matter either. I subsequently solved this problem,
always fundamental in time of adversity, by wearing a
kepi and saluting in military fashion, no, that must be
wrong, I don't know, I had my hat at the end. I never
made the mistake of wearing medals. Some landladies
were in such need of money that they let me in immediately and showed me the room. But I couldn't
come to an agreement with any of them. Finally I
found a basement. With this woman I came to an
agreement at once. My oddities, that's the expression
she used, did not alarm her. She nevertheless insisted
on making the bed and cleaning the room once a week,

instead of once a month as I requested. She told me
that while she was cleaning, which would not take
long, I could wait in the area. She added, with a great
deal of feeling, that she would never put me out in bad
weather. This woman was Greek, I think, or Turkish.
She never spoke about herself. I somehow got the idea
she was a widow or at least that her husband had left
her. She had a strange accent. But so had I with my
way of assimilating the vowels and omitting the
consonants.

Now I didn't know where I was. I had a vague vision,
not a real vision, I didn't see anything, of a big house
five or six stories high, one of a block perhaps. It was
dusk when I got there and I did not pay the same heed
to my surroundings as I might have done if I had
suspected they were to close about me. And by then I
must have lost all hope. It is true that when I left this
house it was a glorious day, but I never look back
when leaving. I must have read somewhere, when I
was small and still read, that it is better not to look
back when leaving. And yet I sometimes did. But
even without looking back it seems to me I should
have seen something when leaving. But there it is. All
I remember is my feet emerging from my shadow, one
after the other. My shoes had stiffened and the sun
brought out the cracks in the leather.

I was comfortable enough in this house, I must say.
Apart from a few rats I was alone in the basement. The
woman did her best to respect our agreement. About
noon she brought me a big tray of food and took away
the tray of the previous day. At the same time she
brought me a clean chamber-pot. The chamber-pot
had a large handle which she slipped over her arm so
that both her hands were free to carry the tray. The
rest of the day I saw no more of her except sometimes

when she peeped in to make sure nothing had happened
to me. Fortunately I did not need affection. From my
bed I saw the feet coming and going on the sidewalk.
Certain evenings, when the weather was fine and I felt
equal to it, I fetched my chair into the area and sat
looking up into the skirts of the women passing by.
Once I sent for a crocus bulb and planted it in the dark
area, in an old pot. It must have been coming up to
spring, it was probably not the right time for it. I left
the pot outside, attached to a string I passed through
the window. In the evening, when the weather was
fine, a little light crept up the wall. Then I sat down
beside the window and pulled on the string to keep the
pot in the light and warmth. That can't have been
easy, I don't see how I managed it. It was probably
not the right thing for it. I manured it as best I could
and pissed on it when the weather was dry. It may not
have been the right thing for it. It sprouted, but never
any flowers, just a wilting stem and a few chlorotic
leaves. I would have liked to have a yellow crocus, or a
hyacinth, but there, it was not to be. She wanted to
take it away, but I told her to leave it. She wanted to
buy me another, but I told her I didn't want another.
What lacerated me most was the din of the newspaper
boys. They went pounding by every day at the same
hours, their heels thudding on the sidewalk, crying
the names of their papers and even the headlines. The
house noises disturbed me less. A little girl, unless it was
a little boy, sang every evening at the same hour,
somewhere above me. For a long time I could not catch
the words. But hearing them day after day I finally
managed to catch a few. Strange words for a little girl,
or a little boy. Was it a song in my head or did it
merely come from without? It was a sort of lullaby, I
believe. It often sent me to sleep, even me. Sometimes

it was a little girl who came. She had long red hair hanging down in two braids. I didn't know who she was. She lingered awhile in the room, then went away without a word. One day I had a visit from a policeman. He said I had to be watched, without explaining why. Suspicious, that was it, he told me I was suspicious. I let him talk. He didn't dare arrest me. Or perhaps he had a kind heart. A priest too, one day I had a visit from a priest. I informed him I belonged to a branch of the reformed church. He asked me what kind of clergyman I would like to see. Yes, there's that about the reformed church, you're lost, it's unavoidable. Perhaps he had a kind heart. He told me to let him know if I ever needed a helping hand. A helping hand! He gave me his name and explained where I could reach him. I should have made a note of it.

One day the woman made me an offer. She said she was in urgent need of cash and that if I could pay her six months in advance she would reduce my rent by one fourth during that period, something of that kind. This had the advantage of saving six weeks' (?) rent and the disadvantage of almost exhausting my small capital. But could you call that a disadvantage? Wouldn't I stay on in any case till my last penny was gone, and even longer, till she put me out? I gave her the money and she gave me a receipt.

One morning, not long after this transaction, I was awakened by a man shaking my shoulder. It could not have been much past eleven. He requested me to get up and leave his house immediately. He was most correct, I must say. His surprise, he said, was no less than mine. It was his house. His property. The Turkish woman had left the day before. But I saw her last night, I said. You must be mistaken, he said, for she brought

the keys to my office no later than yesterday afternoon.
But I just paid her six months' rent in advance, I said.
Get a refund, he said. But I don't even know her name,
I said, let alone her address. You don't know her name?
he said. He must have thought I was lying. I'm sick, I
said, I can't leave like this, without any notice. You're
not so sick as all that, he said. He offered to send for
a taxi, even an ambulance if I preferred. He said he
needed the room immediately for his pig which even as
he spoke was catching cold in a cart before the door
and no one to look after him but a stray urchin whom
he had never set eyes on before and who was probably
busy tormenting him. I asked if he couldn't let me
have another place, any old corner where I could lie
down long enough to recover from the shock and
decide what to do. He said he could not. Don't think
I'm being unkind, he added. I could live here with the
pig, I said, I'd look after him. The long months of
peace, wiped out in an instant! Come now, come now,
he said, get a grip on yourself, be a man, get up, that's
enough. After all it was no concern of his. He had
really been most patient. He must have visited the
basement while I was sleeping.

I felt weak. Perhaps I was. I stumbled in the blinding
light. A bus took me into the country. I sat down in a
field in the sun. But it seems to me that was much later.
I stuck leaves under my hat, all the way round, to
make a shade. The night was cold. I wandered for
hours in the fields. At last I found a heap of dung. The
next day I started back to the city. They made me get
off three buses. I sat down by the roadside and dried
my clothes in the sun. I enjoyed doing that. I said to
myself, There's nothing more to be done now, not a
thing, till they are dry. When they were dry I brushed
them with a brush, I think a kind of curry-comb, that I

found in a stable. Stables have always been my sal-
vation. Then I went to the house and begged a glass of
milk and a slice of bread and butter. They gave me
everything except the butter. May I rest in the stable?
I said. No, they said. I still stank, but with a stink that
pleased me. I much preferred it to my own which
moreover it prevented me from smelling, except a
waft now and then. In the days that followed I took
the necessary steps to recover my money. I don't know
exactly what happened, whether I couldn't find the
address, or whether there was no such address, or
whether the Greek woman was unknown there. I
ransacked my pockets for the receipt, to try and deci-
pher the name. It wasn't there. Perhaps she had taken
it back while I was sleeping. I don't know how long I
wandered thus, resting now in one place, now in
another, in the city and in the country. The city had
suffered many changes. Nor was the country as I
remembered it. The general effect was the same. One
day I caught sight of my son. He was striding along
with a briefcase under his arm. He took off his hat and
bowed and I saw he was as bald as a coot. I was almost
certain it was he. I turned round to gaze after him. He
went bustling along on his duck feet, bowing and
scraping and flourishing his hat left and right. The
insufferable son of a bitch.

One day I met a man I had known in former times.
He lived in a cave by the sea. He had an ass that
grazed winter and summer, over the cliffs, or along the
little tracks leading down to the sea. When the weather
was very bad this ass came down to the cave of his own
accord and sheltered there till the storm was past. So
they had spent many a night huddled together, while
the wind howled and the sea pounded on the shore.
With the help of this ass he could deliver sand, sea-

wrack and shells to the townsfolk, for their gardens. He couldn't carry much at a time, for the ass was old and small and the town was far. But in this way he earned a little money, enough to keep him in tobacco and matches and to buy a piece of bread from time to time. It was during one of these excursions that he met me, in the suburbs. He was delighted to see me, poor man. He begged me to go home with him and spend the night. Stay as long as you like, he said. What's wrong with your ass? I said. Don't mind him, he said, he doesn't know you. I reminded him that I wasn't in the habit of staying more than two or three minutes with anyone and that the sea did not agree with me. He seemed deeply grieved to hear it. So you won't come, he said. But to my amazement I got up on the ass and off we went, in the shade of the red chestnuts springing from the sidewalk. I held the ass by the mane, one hand in front of the other. The little boys jeered and threw stones, but their aim was poor, for they only hit me once, on the hat. A policeman stopped us and accused us of disturbing the peace. My friend replied that we were as nature had made us, the boys too were as nature had made them. It was inevitable, under these conditions, that the peace should be disturbed from time to time. Let us continue on our way, he said, and order will soon be restored throughout your beat. We followed the quiet, dustwhite inland roads with their hedges of hawthorn and fuchsia and their footpaths fringed with wild grass and daisies. Night fell. The ass carried me right to the mouth of the cave, for in the dark I could not have found my way down the path winding steeply to the sea. Then he climbed back to his pasture.

I don't know how long I stayed there. The cave was nicely arranged, I must say. I treated my crablice with

salt water and seaweed, but a lot of nits must have
survived. I put compresses of seaweed on my skull,
which gave me great relief, but not for long. I lay in
the cave and sometimes looked out at the horizon. I
saw above me a vast trembling expanse without islands
or promontories. At night a light shone into the cave at
regular intervals. It was here I found the phial in my
pocket. It was not broken, for the glass was not real
glass. I thought Mr. Weir had confiscated all my belongings. My host was out most of the time. He fed me
on fish. It is easy for a man, a proper man, to live in a
cave, far from everybody. He invited me to stay as
long as I liked. If I preferred to be alone he would
gladly prepare another cave for me further on. He
would bring me food every day and drop in from time
to time to make sure I was all right and needed nothing.
He was kind. Unfortunately I did not need kindness.
You wouldn't know of a lake dwelling? I said. I
couldn't bear the sea, its splashing and heaving, its
tides and general convulsiveness. The wind at least
sometimes stops. My hands and feet felt as though they
were full of ants. This kept me awake for hours on end.
If I stayed here something awful would happen to me,
I said, and a lot of good that would do me. You'd get
drowned, he said. Yes, I said, or jump off the cliff. And
to think I couldn't live anywhere else, he said, in my
cabin in the mountains I was wretched. Your cabin in
the mountains? I said. He repeated the story of his
cabin in the mountains, I had forgotten it, it was as
though I were hearing it for the first time. I asked him
if he still had it. He replied he had not seen it since the
day he fled from it, but that he believed it was still
there, a little decayed no doubt. But when he urged
me to take the key I refused, saying I had other
plans. You will always find me here, he said, if you

ever need me. Ah people. He gave me his knife.

What he called his cabin in the mountains was a sort of wooden shed. The door had been removed, for firewood, or for some other purpose. The glass had disappeared from the window. The roof had fallen in at several places. The interior was divided, by the remains of a partition, into two unequal parts. If there had been any furniture it was gone. The vilest acts had been committed on the ground and against the walls. The floor was strewn with excrements, both human and animal, with condoms and vomit. In a cowpad a heart had been traced, pierced by an arrow. And yet there was nothing to attract tourists. I noticed the remains of abandoned nosegays. They had been greedily gathered, carried for miles, then thrown away, because they were cumbersome or already withered. This was the dwelling to which I had been offered the key.

The scene was the familiar one of grandeur and desolation.

Nevertheless it was a roof over my head. I rested on a bed of ferns, gathered at great labour with my own hands. One day I couldn't get up. The cow saved me. Goaded by the icy mist she came in search of shelter. It was probably not the first time. She can't have seen me. I tried to suck her, without much success. Her udder was covered with dung. I took off my hat and, summoning all my energy, began to milk her into it. The milk fell to the ground and was lost, but I said to myself, No matter, it's free. She dragged me across the floor, stopping from time to time only to kick me. I didn't know our cows too could be so inhuman. She must have recently been milked. Clutching the dug with one hand I kept my hat under it with the other. But in the end she prevailed. For she dragged me across the threshold and out into the giant streaming ferns, where I was forced to let go.

As I drank the milk I reproached myself with what I had done. I could no longer count on this cow and she would warn the others. More master of myself I might have made a friend of her. She would have come every day, perhaps accompanied by other cows. I might have learnt to make butter, even cheese. But I said to myself, No, all is for the best.

Once on the road it was all downhill. Soon there were carts, but they all refused to take me up. In other clothes, with another face, they might have taken me up. I must have changed since my expulsion from the basement. The face notably seemed to have attained its climacteric. The humble, ingenuous smile would no longer come, nor the expression of candid misery, showing the stars and the distaff. I summoned them, but they would not come. A mask of dirty old hairy leather, with two holes and a slit, it was too far gone for the old trick of please your honour and God reward you and pity upon me. It was disastrous. What would I crawl with in future? I lay down on the side of the road and began to writhe each time I heard a cart approaching. That was so they would not think I was sleeping or resting. I tried to groan, Help! Help! But the tone that came out was that of polite conversation. My hour was not yet come and I could no longer groan. The last time I had cause to groan I had groaned as well as ever, and no heart within miles of me to melt. What was to become of me? I said to myself, I'll learn again. I lay down across the road at a narrow place, so that the carts could not pass without passing over my body, with one wheel at least, or two if there were four. But the day came when, looking round me, I was in the suburbs, and from there to the old haunts it was not far, beyond the stupid hope of rest or less pain.

So I covered the lower part of my face with a black rag and went and begged at a sunny corner. For it seemed to me my eyes were not completely spent, thanks perhaps to the dark glasses my tutor had given me. He had given me the *Ethics* of Geulincz. They were a man's glasses, I was a child. They found him dead, crumpled up in the water closet, his clothes in awful disorder, struck down by an infarctus. Ah what peace. The *Ethics* had his name (Ward) on the fly-leaf, the glasses had belonged to him. The bridge, at the time I am speaking of, was of brass wire, of the kind used to hang pictures and big mirrors, and two long black ribbons served as wings. I wound them round my ears and then down under my chin where I tied them together. The lenses had suffered, from rubbing in my pocket against each other and against the other objects there. I thought Mr. Weir had confiscated all my belongings. But I had no further need of these glasses and used them merely to soften the glare of the sun. I should never have mentioned them. The rag gave me a lot of trouble. I got it in the end from the lining of my greatcoat, no, I had no greatcoat now, of my coat then. The result was a grey rag rather than a black, perhaps even chequered, but I had to make do with it. Till afternoon I held my face raised towards the southern sky, then towards the western till night. The bowl gave me a lot of trouble. I couldn't use my hat because of my skull. As for holding out my hand, that was quite out of the question. So I got a tin and hung it from a button of my greatcoat, what's the matter with me, of my coat, at pubis level. It did not hang plumb, it leaned respectfully towards the passer-by, he had only to drop his mite. But that obliged him to come up close to me, he

was in danger of touching me. In the end I got a
bigger tin, a kind of big tin box, and I placed it on the
sidewalk at my feet. But people who give alms don't
much care to toss them, there's something contemptuous
about this gesture which is repugnant to sensitive
natures. To say nothing of their having to aim. They
are prepared to give, but not for their gift to go
rolling under the passing feet or under the passing
wheels, to be picked up perhaps by some undeserving
person. So they don't give. There are those, to be sure,
who stoop, but generally speaking people who give
alms don't much care to stoop. What they like above
all is to sight the wretch from afar, get ready their
penny, drop it in their stride and hear the God bless
you dying away in the distance. Personally I never
said that, nor anything like it, I wasn't much of a be-
liever, but I did make a noise with my mouth. In the
end I got a kind of board or tray and tied it to my
neck and waist. It jutted out just at the right height,
pocket height, and its edge was far enough from my
person for the coin to be bestowed without danger.
Some days I strewed it with flowers, petals, buds and
that herb which men call fleabane, I believe, in a word
whatever I could find. I didn't go out of my way to
look for them, but all the pretty things of this description that came my way were for the board. They
must have thought I loved nature. Most of the time I
looked up at the sky, but without focusing it, for why
focus it? Most of the time it was a mixture of white,
blue and grey, and then at evening all the evening
colours. I felt it weighing softly on my face, I rubbed
my face against it, one cheek after the other, turning
my head from side to side. Now and then to rest my
neck I dropped my head on my chest. Then I could see
the board in the distance, a haze of many colours. I

leaned against the wall, but without nonchalance, I shifted my weight from one foot to the other and my hands clutched the lapels of my coat. To beg with your hands in your pockets makes a bad impression, it irritates the workers, especially in winter. You should never wear gloves either. There were guttersnipes who swept away all I had earned, under cover of giving me a coin. It was to buy sweets. I unbuttoned my trousers discreetly to scratch myself. I scratched myself in an upward direction, with four nails. I pulled on the hairs, to get relief. It passed the time, time flew when I scratched myself. Real scratching is superior to masturbation, in my opinion. One can masturbate up to the age of seventy, and even beyond, but in the end it becomes a mere habit. Whereas to scratch myself properly I would have needed a dozen hands. I itched all over, on the privates, in the bush up to the navel, under the arms, in the arse, and then patches of eczema and psoriasis that I could set raging merely by thinking of them. It was in the arse I had the most pleasure, I stuck in my forefinger up to the knuckle. Later, if I had to shit, the pain was atrocious. But I hardly shat any more. Now and then a flying machine flew by, sluggishly it seemed to me. Often at the end of the day I discovered the legs of my trousers all wet. That must have been the dogs. I personally pissed very little. If by chance the need came on me a little squirt in my fly was enough to relieve it. Once at my post I did not leave it till nightfall. I had no appetite, God tempered the wind to me. After work I bought a bottle of milk and drank it in the evening in the shed. Better still, I got a little boy to buy it for me, always the same, they wouldn't serve me, I don't know why. I gave him a penny for his pains. One day I witnessed a strange scene. Normally I didn't see a great deal. I didn't hear a great deal either. I didn't pay attention. Strictly speaking I wasn't there. Strictly speaking I believe I've never been anywhere. But that day I must have come back. For some time past a sound had been scarifying me. I did not investigate the cause, for I said to myself, It's going to stop. But as it did not stop I had no choice but to find out the cause. It was a man perched on the roof of a car and haranguing the passers-by. That at least was my interpretation. He was bellowing so loud that snatches of his discourse reached my ears. Union . . . brothers . . . Marx . . . capital . . . bread and butter . . . love. It was all Greek to me. The car was drawn up against the kerb, just in front of me, I saw the orator from behind. All of a sudden he turned and pointed at me, as at an exhibit. Look at this down and out, he vociferated, this leftover. If he doesn't go down on all fours, it's for fear of being impounded. Old, lousy, rotten, ripe for the muckheap. And there are a thousand like him, worse than him, ten thousand, twenty thousand—. A voice, Thirty thousand. Every day you pass them by, resumed the orator, and when you have backed a winner you fling them a farthing. Do you ever think? The voice, God forbid. A penny, resumed the orator, tuppence—. The voice, thruppence. It never enters your head, resumed the orator, that your charity is a crime, an incentive to slavery, stultification and organized murder. Take a good look at this living corpse. You may say it's his own fault. Ask him if it's his own fault. The voice, Ask him yourself. Then he bent forward and took me to task. I had perfected my board. It now consisted of two boards hinged together, which enabled me, when my work was done, to fold it and carry it under my arm. I liked doing little odd jobs. So I took off the rag, pocketed the few coins I had earned, untied the board, folded it and put it under my

arm. Do you hear me, you crucified bastard! cried the
orator. Then I went away, although it was still light.
But generally speaking it was a quiet corner, busy but
not overcrowded, thriving and well-frequented. He
must have been a religious fanatic, I could find no
other explanation. Perhaps he was an escaped lunatic.
He had a nice face, a little on the red side.

I did not work every day. I had practically no
expenses. I even managed to put a little aside, for my
very last days. The days I did not work I spent lying in
the shed. The shed was on a private estate, or what
had once been a private estate, on the riverside. This
estate, the main entrance to which opened on a
narrow, dark and silent street, was enclosed with a
wall, except of course on the river front, which marked
its northern boundary for a distance of about thirty
yards. From the last quays beyond the water the eyes
rose to a confusion of low houses, wasteland, hoardings,
chimneys, steeples and towers. A kind of parade
ground was also to be seen, where soldiers played
football all the year round. Only the ground-floor
windows—no, I can't. The estate seemed abandoned.
The gates were locked and the paths overgrown with
grass. Only the ground-floor windows had shutters.
The others were sometimes lit at night, faintly, now one,
now another. At least that was my impression.
Perhaps it was reflected light. In this shed, the day I
adopted it, I found a boat, upside down. I righted it,
chocked it up with stones and pieces of wood, took
out the thwarts and made my bed inside. The rats had
difficulty in getting at me, because of the bulge of the
hull. And yet they longed to. Just think of it, living
flesh, for in spite of everything I was still living flesh.
I had lived too long among rats, in my chance dwell-
ings, to share the dread they inspire in the vulgar. I

even had a soft spot in my heart for them. They came with such confidence towards me, it seemed without the least repugnance. They made their toilet with catlike gestures. Toads at evening, motionless for hours, lap flies from the air. They like to squat where cover ends and open air begins, they favour thresholds. But I had to contend now with water rats, exceptionally lean and ferocious. So I made a kind of lid with stray boards. It's incredible the number of boards I've come across in my lifetime, I never needed a board but there it was, I had only to stoop and pick it up. I liked doing little odd jobs, no, not particularly, I didn't mind. It completely covered the boat, I'm referring again to the lid. I pushed it a little towards the stern, climbed into the boat by the bow, crawled to the stern, raised my feet and pushed the lid back towards the bow till it covered me completely. But what did my feet push against? They pushed against a cross-bar I nailed to the lid for that purpose, I liked these little odd jobs. But it was better to climb into the boat by the stern and pull back the lid with my hands till it completely covered me, then push it forward in the same way when I wanted to get out. As holds for my hands I planted two spikes just where I needed them. These little odds and ends of carpentry, if I may so describe it, carried out with whatever tools and material I chanced to find, gave me a certain pleasure. I knew it would soon be the end, so I played the part, you know, the part of—how shall I say, I don't know. I was comfortable enough in this boat, I must say. The lid fitted so well I had to pierce a hole. It's no good closing your eyes, you must leave them open in the dark, that is my opinion. I am not speaking of sleep, I am speaking of what I believe is called waking. In any case, I slept very little at this period, I wasn't sleepy, or I was too

sleepy, I don't know, or I was afraid, I don't know.
Flat then on my back I saw nothing except, dimly, just
above my head, through the tiny chinks, the grey light
of the shed. To see nothing at all, no, that's too much.
I heard faintly the cries of the gulls ravening about the
mouth of the sewer near by. In a spew of yellow foam,
if my memory serves me right, the filth gushed into the
river and the slush of birds above screaming with
hunger and fury. I heard the lapping of water against
the slip and against the bank and the other sound, so
different, of open wave, I heard it too. I too, when I
moved, felt less boat than wave, or so it seemed to me,
and my stillness was the stillness of eddies. That may
seem impossible. The rain too, I often heard it, for it
often rained. Sometimes a drop, falling through the
roof of the shed, exploded on me. All that composed a
rather liquid world. And then of course there was the
voice of the wind or rather those, so various, of its
playthings. But what does it amount to? Howling,
soughing, moaning, sighing. What I would have liked
was hammer strokes, bang bang bang, clanging in the
desert. I let farts to be sure, but hardly ever a real
crack, they oozed out with a sucking noise, melted in
the mighty never. I don't know how long I stayed there.
I was very snug in my box, I must say. It seemed to
me I had grown more independent of recent years.
That no one came any more, that no one could come
any more to ask me if I was all right and needed
nothing, distressed me then but little. I was all right,
yes, quite so, and the fear of getting worse was less with
me. As for my needs, they had dwindled as it were to
my dimensions and become, if I may say so, of so exquisite a quality as to exclude all thought of succour.
To know I had a being, however faint and false, outside of me, had once had the power to stir my heart.

You become unsociable, it's inevitable. It's enough to
make you wonder sometimes if you are on the right
planet. Even the words desert you, it's as bad as that.
Perhaps it's the moment when the vessels stop com-
municating, you know, the vessels. There you are still
between the two murmurs, it must be the same old
song as ever, but Christ you wouldn't think so. There
were times when I wanted to push away the lid and
get out of the boat and couldn't, I was so indolent and
weak, so content deep down where I was. I felt them
hard upon me, the icy, tumultuous streets, the terrify-
ing faces, the noises that slash, pierce, claw, bruise. So
I waited till the desire to shit, or even to piss, lent me
wings. I did not want to dirty my nest! And yet it
sometimes happened, and even more and more often.
Arched and rigid I edged down my trousers and turned
a little on my side, just enough to free the hole. To
contrive a little kingdom, in the midst of the universal
muck, then shit on it, ah that was me all over. The
excrements were me too, I know, I know, but all the
same. Enough, enough, the next thing I was having
visions, I who never did, except sometimes in my sleep,
who never had, real visions, I'd remember, except
perhaps as a child, my myth will have it so. I knew they
were visions because it was night and I was alone in my
boat. What else could they have been? So I was in my
boat and gliding on the waters. I didn't have to row,
the ebb was carrying me out. Anyway I saw no oars,
they must have taken them away. I had a board, the
remains of a thwart perhaps, which I used when I
came too close to the bank, or when a pier came bearing down on me or a barge at its moorings. There were
stars in the sky, quite a few. I didn't know what the
weather was doing, I was neither cold nor warm and
all seemed calm. The banks receded more and more,

it was inevitable, soon I saw them no more. The lights grew fainter and fewer as the river widened. There on the land men were sleeping, bodies were gathering strength for the toil and joys of the morrow. The boat was not gliding now, it was tossing, buffeted by the choppy waters of the bay. All seemed calm and yet foam was washing aboard. Now the sea air was all about me, I had no other shelter than the land, and what does it amount to, the shelter of the land, at such a time. I saw the beacons, four in all, including a lightship. I knew them well, even as a child I had known them well. It was evening, I was with my father on a height, he held my hand. I would have liked him to draw me close with a gesture of protective love, but his mind was on other things. He also taught me the names of the mountains. But to have done with these visions I also saw the lights of the buoys, the sea seemed full of them, red and green and to my surprise even yellow. And on the slopes of the mountain, now rearing its unbroken bulk behind the town, the fires turned from gold to red, from red to gold. I knew what it was, it was the gorse burning. How often I had set a match to it myself, as a child. And hours later, back in my home, before I climbed into bed, I watched from my high window the fires I had lit. That night then, all aglow with distant fires, on sea, on land and in the sky, I drifted with the currents and the tides. I noticed that my hat was tied, with a string I suppose, to my buttonhole. I got up from my seat in the stern and a great clanking was heard. That was the chain. One end was fastened to the bow and the other round my waist. I must have pierced a hole beforehand in the floor-boards, for there I was down on my knees prying out the plug with my knife. The hole was small and the water rose slowly. It would take a good half hour, everything included, barring accidents. Back now in the stern-sheets, my legs stretched out, my back well propped against the sack stuffed with grass I used as a cushion, I swallowed my calmative. The sea, the sky, the mountains and the islands closed in and crushed me in a mighty systole, then scattered to the uttermost confines of space. The memory came faint and cold of the story I might have told, a story in the likeness of my life, I mean without the courage to end or the strength to go on.

—Translated by RICHARD SEAVER
in collaboration with the author.